Other books in the series include:

God's Little Book of Encouragement
(David Marshall)

God's Little Book of Peace
(David Marshall)

God's Little Book of Praise for Women
(Mary Barrett)

God's Little Book of Prayer
(Richard Daly)

God's Little Book of Promises
(David Marshall)

The world is tired of
Christians who say they
have the right beliefs
and right values but in
whom there is no grace.
Grasp grace!
Be gracious!

'There is no fear in love.
But perfect love drives out fear.'

1 John 4:18.

You are beloved of God.
What can you put on
your CV to top that?

'How great is the love the Father
has lavished on us.'

1 John 3:1.

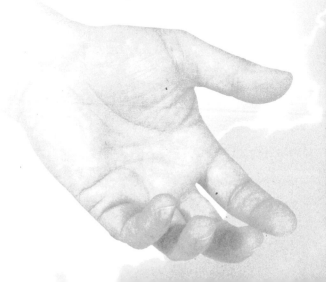

The fruit of the Spirit is the fruit of grace.

'The fruit of the Spirit is love, joy, peace, patience, kindness, goodness, faithfulness, gentleness and self-control.'

Galatians 5:22, 23.

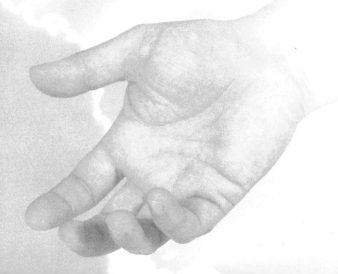

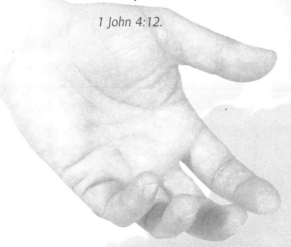

The best argument for
Christianity is Christians:
their joy, their certainty,
their graciousness.

'No one has ever seen God;
but if we love one another,
God lives in us and his love
is made complete in us.'

1 John 4:12.

The world says,
'There's no such thing
as a free lunch.
Quid pro quo.'
God says, 'Come!
No charge!'

' "Come, all you who are thirsty,
come to the waters." '

Isaiah 55:1.

By grace, says the New Testament, you have become alive to God. And that gives you a reason to hope.

'There is surely a future hope for you, and your hope will not be cut off.'

Proverbs 23:18.

God loves to lavish
grace on the left-out,
the used-up
and the put-down.

' "I know the plans I have for you,"
declares the Lord, "plans to prosper
you and not to harm you, plans to
give you hope and a future." '

Jeremiah 29:11.

Brought up in luxury, Moses was heir to the kingdom. But the fact that he was heir to *God's* kingdom – as we are – mattered more to him.

'By faith Moses, . . . regarded disgrace for the sake of Christ as of greater value than the treasures of Egypt.'

Hebrews 11:24-26.

Grace recruits more for
eternity than zeal,
eloquence or learning
ever did.

'Whoever drinks the water
I give him will never thirst.
Indeed, the water I give
him will become in him a
stream of water welling
up to eternal life.'

John 4:14.

The invitation
of grace is 'Come!'

'Whoever comes to me
I will never drive away.'

John 6:37.

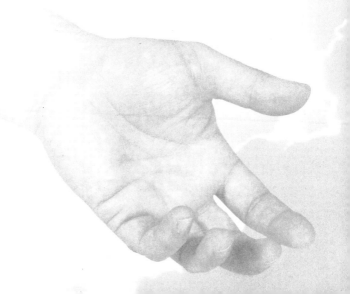

God's love: no limits.
God's grace: no measure.
God's power: no boundaries.

'While he was still a long way off,
his father saw him and was
filled with compassion for him;
he ran to his son, threw his arms
around him and kissed him.'

Luke 15:20.

In the cross God declares
his hatred of sin and
his limitless love of
the sinner.

'For God was pleased to have
all his fullness dwell in [Jesus],
and through him to reconcile
to himself all things . . . by
making peace through his
blood, shed on the cross.'

Colossians 1:19, 20.

Help your friends to
bear their burdens! It
will multiply grace –
and put your own
troubles into
perspective.

'Share each other's troubles
and problems, and in this
way obey the law of Christ.'

Galatians 6:2, NLT.

Carpe diem! Seize the day!
Today is a gift from God!
Take it and squeeze every
ounce of joy out of it.

'This is the day the
Lord has made;
let us rejoice and
be glad in it.'

Psalm 118:24.

With God there are no 'grey days'. When high hopes take a hike and dreams seem to be turning into nightmares, when good intentions get lost in a comedy of errors, it's time to count your blessings.

'Great is his faithfulness; his mercies begin afresh each day.'

Lamentations 3:23, NLT.

We need to be so filled
full of the life of Jesus
that, in touching the
world, instead of its
infecting us we infect it!

'I'm not saying that . . .
I have it made.
But I am well on my way,
reaching out for Christ,
who has so wondrously
reached out for me.'

Philippians 3:13, MGE.

Mired in the past?
It's time to move on!

'I've wiped the slate of
all your wrongdoings.
There's nothing left of your sins.
Come back to me, come back.
I've redeemed you.'

Isaiah 44:22, MGE.

The love of God is
beyond question.
The question is,
'Do we seek him?'

'The earth is filled with
your love, O Lord;
teach me your decrees.'

Psalm 119:64.

In your life, are you
sowing seeds – or just
scaring the birds?

'At the proper time,
we will reap a harvest
if we do not give up.'

Galatians 6:9.

If God had signs in his
shop they would say,
'Please touch.'

'Give thanks to the Lord,
for he is good.
His love endures forever.'

Psalm 136:1.

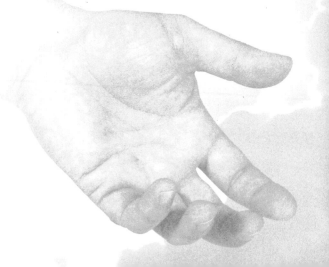

In a contagious world
Jesus did not call upon
us to live in quarantine.
He called us to be
a hospital.

'Go and make disciples of all
nations, baptising them . . .
and teaching them to
obey everything I
have commanded.'

Matthew 28:19, 20.

He is Lord of the second chance.

'Great is your love toward me;
you have delivered me
from the depths.'

Psalm 86:13.

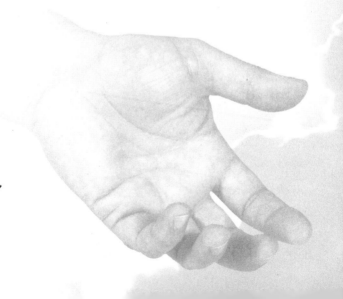

Are you a loser or a
learner? With God as
your source, you've got
everything you need
to make it.

'His divine power has given
us everything we need.'

2 Peter 1:3.

Love of God is the root,
love of our neighbour
is the fruit of the
Tree of Life.

'The Lord is gracious
and compassionate,
slow to anger and
rich in love.'

Psalm 145:8.

Grace is the key to
unlock the heavy doors.

'The Lord's unfailing love
surrounds the man
who trusts in him.'

Psalm 32:10.

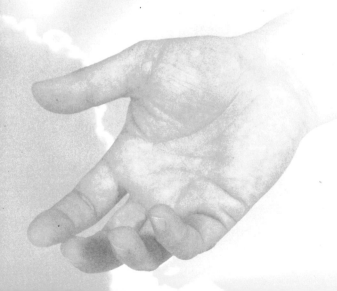

God says, 'Come home!
Stop hiding!' It is the
cry of grace.

'See how close his salvation is
to those who fear him? . . .
Love and Truth meet in the street,
Right Living and Whole Living
embrace!'

Psalm 85:12, 13, MGE.

Feeling anxious and afraid?
God has everything
under control.

' "Do not fear, for I am with you;
do not be dismayed,
for I am your God." '

Isaiah 41:10.

When things fall through
or fizzle out, and people
walk away, remember,
God is holding the
door open. . . .

'See, I have placed before
you an open door that
no one can shut.'

Revelation 3:8.

Never lose sight of
your final destination!
There are *eternal*
rewards!

'And now the prize awaits me –
the crown of righteousness.'

2 Timothy 4:8, NLT.

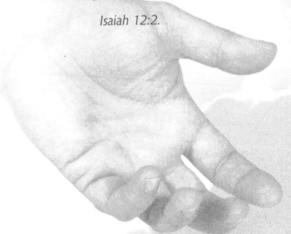

If you're worrying,
it means you've
forgotten who's
in charge.

'"I will trust and not be afraid.
The Lord, the Lord, is my strength
and my song; he has become
my salvation."'

Isaiah 12:2.

Grace is all. It is the
nub of the universe.
We walk by it, we
breathe it, we live it
and we die in it.

'Grace was given to us in Christ Jesus
before the beginning of time, but
it has now been revealed through
the appearing of our Saviour,
Christ Jesus, who has destroyed
death and brought life and
immortality to light through
the gospel.'

2 Timothy 1:9, 10.

Grace is power,
not just pardon.

'May our Lord Jesus Christ
himself and God our Father,
who loved us and by his grace gave
us eternal encouragement . . .
encourage your hearts.'

2 Thessalonians 2:16, 17.

Just as apology must
precede reconciliation,
so repentance must
precede pardon.
God is ready
when you are!

'You are a forgiving God,
gracious and passionate,
slow to anger and
abounding in love.'

Nehemiah 9:17.

The Christian life
starts with grace,
continues with grace,
and ends with grace.
It is grace first,
last and for ever.

'The grace of our Lord was
poured out on me abundantly,
along with the faith and love
that are in Christ Jesus.'

1 Timothy 1:14.

Grace is not a
decoration for heroes –
but to help heal
the spiritually sick.

Jesus said, ' "It is not the healthy
who need a doctor, but the sick.
I have not come to call the
righteous, but sinners." '

Mark 2:17.

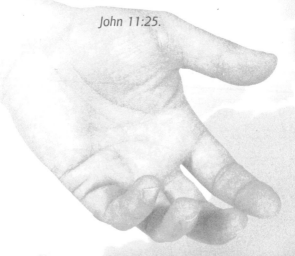

Those who die in God's grace go no further than God does.

Jesus said, ' "I am the resurrection and the life. He who believes in me will live, even though he dies; and whoever lives and believes in me will never die." '

John 11:25.

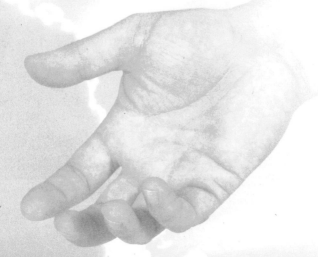

Life is too short to
spend it as an inmate
of the prison of your
previous mistakes.

'You, my brothers, . . .
were called to be free.'

Galatians 5:13.

Grace is the best means of outreach.

'Use your heads as you live
and work among outsiders.
Don't miss a trick. Make the
most of every opportunity.
Be gracious in your speech.
The goal is to bring out the
best in others in a conversation,
not put them down,
not cut them out.'

Colossians 4:5, 6, MGE.

The consequences of grace are not just posthumous!
The grace-life starts here, *on earth*.

'All over the world this gospel is bearing fruit and growing, just as it has been doing among you since the day you heard it and understood God's grace in all its truth.'

Colossians 1:6.

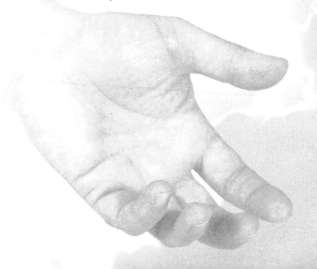

Grace is not just for receiving – it's for giving!

'I became a servant of this gospel by the gift of God's grace given me through the working of his power.'

Ephesians 3:7.

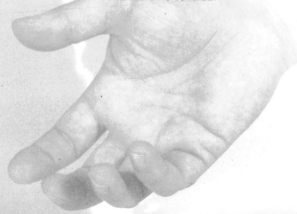

Grace brings about
internal change. It enters
by the ear to transform
the heart.

'When you attempt to live by your
own religious plans and projects,
you are cut off from Christ,
you fall out of grace.'

Galatians 5:4, 5, MGE.

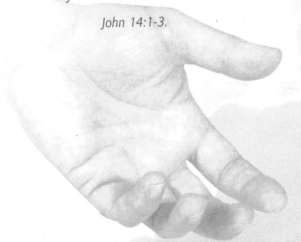

The best – the *very* best –
benefits of grace are
yet to be.

‘ "Do not let your hearts be troubled.
Trust in God; trust also in me. . . .
If I go and prepare a place for you,
I will come back and take
you to be with me." ’

John 14:1-3.

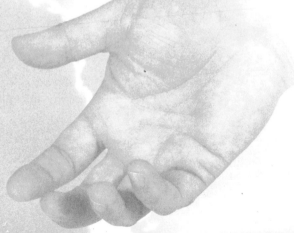

Our salvation is as sure
as God's most solemn
promise.

'If the inheritance depends on the law,
then it no longer depends on a promise;
but God in his grace gave it . . .
through a promise.'

Galatians 3:18.

The result of embracing grace?
Gracious behaviour.

'I worked harder than
all of them – yet not I,
but the grace of God
that was with me.'

1 Corinthians 15:10.

The triple security
of grace.

' "My sheep listen to my voice;
I know them, and they follow me.
I give them eternal life, and they
shall never perish; no one can
snatch them out of my hand.
My Father, who has given them
to me, is greater than all; no
one can snatch them out of my
Father's hand." '

John 10:27-29.

The pen has always been
mightier than the sword.
And the words of Jesus
have, for twenty centuries,
been the food of eternity.

Peter said, ' "Lord,
to whom would we go?
You alone have the words
that give eternal life." '

John 6:68, NLT.

Those who live with
serenity do so by the
assurance
of grace.

'You will keep in perfect peace
him whose mind is steadfast,
because he trusts in you.'

Isaiah 26:3.

The response that springs from grace is – discipleship.

'Shall we go on sinning so
that grace may increase?
By no means! We died to sin;
how can we live in it any longer?'

Romans 6:1, 2.

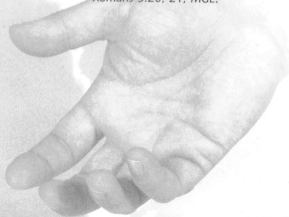

Christ has unbolted
the door of grace –
and we are inside.

'Sin didn't, and doesn't, have a
chance in competition with the
aggressive forgiveness we call *grace*.
When it's sin versus grace,
grace wins hands down.'

Romans 5:20, 21, MGE.

. . . and grace can strike
us right in the midst of
pain, restlessness and
meaninglessness!
That's how God works!

'If death got the upper
hand through one man's wrongdoing,
can you imagine the breathtaking
recovery life makes . . . in those who
grasp with both hands this wildly
extravagant life-gift . . .
that the one man
Jesus Christ provides?'

Romans 5:18, MGE.

Grace – the undeserved favour of God to mankind.

'If the many died by the trespass
of the one man, how much more did
God's grace and the gift that came
by the grace of the one man,
Jesus Christ, overflow
to the many!'

Romans 5:15.

Grace = glory begun.
Glory = grace perfected.

'Grow in the grace and
knowledge of our Lord
and Saviour Jesus Christ.
To him be glory both
now and forever!'

2 Peter 3:18.

You have a great need
for Christ.
You have a great Christ
for your need.

'I am sure that God, who began the
good work within you, will continue
his work until it is finally finished on
that day when Christ Jesus comes
back again.'

Philippians 1:6, NLT.

Grace is costly –
because it costs a
man his life.

'Greater love has no one than this,
that he lay down his life
for his friends.'

John 15:13.

If there were such a
thing as 'cheap grace'
it would be grace
without discipleship,
talk without action.

'Isn't it obvious that
God-talk without God-acts
is outrageous nonsense?'

James 2:17, 18, MGE.

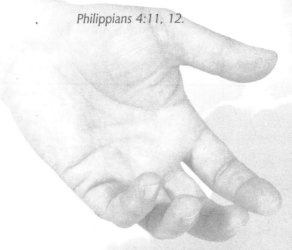

Knowing Jesus is
the secret of grace.

'I have learned to be content
whatever the circumstances.
I know what it is to be in need,
and I know what it is to have plenty.
I have learned the secret of being
content in any and every situation.'

Philippians 4:11, 12.

There is no greater
grace than the grace
with which we stand
surrounded.

'Through our Lord Jesus Christ . . .
we have gained access by faith into
this grace in which we now stand.
And we rejoice in the hope of
the glory of God.'

Romans 5:1, 2.

God's grace is infinite – and has at least three dimensions!

'I pray that you, being rooted and established in love, may have power . . . to grasp how wide and long and high and deep is the love of Christ, and to know this love that surpasses knowledge.'

Ephesians 3:17-19.

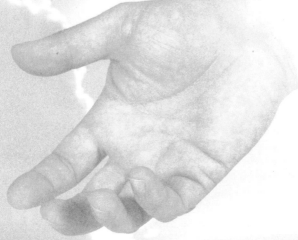

You can advance farther in grace in one hour of trial than in years of ease.

'We want you to know about the grace that God has given. . . . Out of the most severe trial [has come] overflowing joy.'

2 Corinthians 8:1, 2.

The grace price-tag says,
'Worth the life
of my Son.'

'Put your hope in the Lord,
for with the Lord is unfailing love
and with him is full redemption.'

Psalm 130:7.

Love for God and
obedience to God are
so completely involved
in each other that each
one implies the other.

'Here's how we can be sure that
we know God in the right way:
Keep his commandments.
If someone claims, "I know him well!"
but doesn't keep his commandments,
he's obviously a liar. His life doesn't
match his words.'

1 John 2:3, 4, MGE.

God does not love us
because we are valuable.
We are valuable because
God loves us.

'What marvellous love the Father
has extended to us! Just look at it –
we are called children of God!
That's who we really are!'

1 John 3:1, MGE.

God is the most
approachable Person
you have ever
heard of.

'Seek the Lord while you can find him.
Call on him now while he is near.'

Isaiah 55:6, NLT.

Your name –
engraved on his hand.
He loves you!
He will never
forget you!

God says, 'See, I have written
your name on my hand.'

Isaiah 49:16, NLT.

God notices things even
your mother never
saw in you.

'Can a mother forget her nursing
child? Can she feel no love
for a child that she has borne?
But even if that were possible,
I would not forget you!'

Isaiah 49:15, NLT.

. . . The single most
violated commandment
in all Scripture?
God wants your
attention!

'Dear friends,
be quick to listen,
slow to speak. . . .'

James 1:19, NLT.

Not 'cheap grace'!
The price of grace
was Calvary.

'He was wounded and
crushed for our sins.
He was beaten that we
might have peace.
He was whipped, and
we were healed!'

Isaiah 53:5, NLT.

Knock –
and enter God's
place of peace.

'God's a safe-house
for the battered, a sanctuary
during bad times.
On the moment you arrive,
you relax; you're never
sorry you knocked.'

Psalm 9:9, MGE.

The way of prayer is the way of grace.

'If my people,
who are called by my name,
will humble themselves and pray
and seek my face and turn from
their wicked ways, then will I hear
from heaven and will forgive their
sin and will heal their land.'

2 Chronicles 7:14.

He is a God who *notices*.
Every detail of your life
is of immense interest
to God.

'O Lord, you have searched me
and you know me. . . .
You perceive my thoughts
from afar.'

Psalm 139:1, 2.

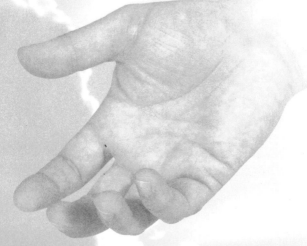

Grace is
never assertive.

'The wisdom that comes from
heaven is first of all pure.
It is also peace loving,
gentle at all times, and
willing to yield to others.'

James 3:17, NLT.

Love gives. Giving is to love what eating is to hunger.

'Dear brothers and sisters, what's the use of saying you have faith if you don't prove it by your actions? . . . Faith that doesn't show itself by good deeds is no faith at all.'

James 2:14, 17, NLT.

Walk with God
and learn the
'unforced rhythms'
of his grace.

'Are you tired? Worn out?
Burned out on religion?
Come to me. Get away with me and
you'll recover your life. I'll show you
how to take a real rest. Walk with me
and work with me – watch how I do it.
Learn the unforced rhythms of grace.'

Matthew 11:28-30, MGE.

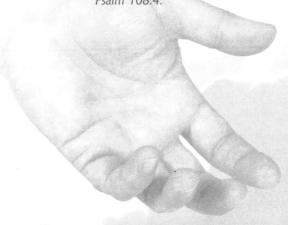

God sees who we
are intended to be
and who we will
one day become.

'Great is your love,
higher than the heavens;
your faithfulness reaches
to the skies.'

Psalm 108:4.

God sees with utter
clarity who you are –
and loves you anyway.

'When I called,
you answered me;
you made me bold
and stouthearted.'

Psalm 138:3.

God's love and grace
are your ultimate
defence.

'In your love you kept me
from the pit of destruction;
you have put all my sins
behind your back.'

Isaiah 38:17.

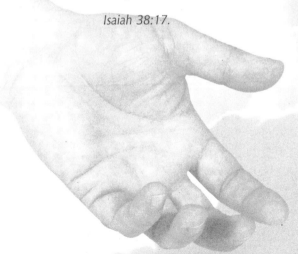

Look into the face of
the Father –
and you will see
yourself reflected
in his eyes.

'Whoever touches you
touches the apple of his eye.'

Zechariah 2:8.

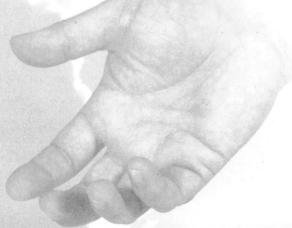

God doesn't love you
because he has to.
He loves you
because he wants to.
And he loves you
to death!

'For God so loved the world that
he gave his one and only Son,
that whoever believes
in him shall not perish
but have eternal life.'

John 3:16.

Do not confuse
sinfulness with
worthlessness.
It's a wonderful thing
that God thinks you're
worth dying for.

'Show the wonder of
your great love. . . .
Keep me as the
apple of your eye;
hide me in the
shadow of your wings.'

Psalm 17:7, 8, NIV.

Grace is the answer –
when the only way out
is through.

'Though you have made me see
troubles, many and bitter,
you will restore my life again;
from the depths of the earth
you will again bring me up.'

Psalm 71:20.

Deliverance *from* our
troubles, usually means
that God
first joins us *in* them.

'The righteous cry out,
and the Lord hears them;
he delivers them from
all their troubles.'

Psalm 34:17.

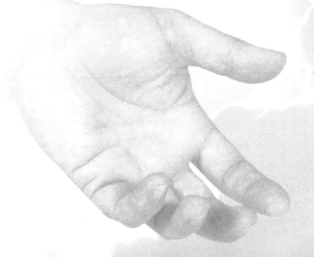

Removing spots and
blemishes is almost
never pain-free.

'Turn to me and
be gracious to me,
for I am lonely and afflicted.'

Psalm 25:16.

The more we depend
on God the more
dependable
we find he is.

' "If you will hold on to me
for dear life," says God,
"I'll get you out of any trouble.
I'll give you the best of care
if you'll only get to know
and trust me." '

Psalm 91:14, 15, MGE.

There is one friend you *can* depend on.

'Even though others
succumb all around, . . .
you'll stand untouched, . . .
yes, because God's your refuge,
the High God your
own home.'

Psalm 91:8-10, MGE.

The God of grace is in your corner.

God's 'huge outstretched arms protect you – under them you're perfectly safe; his arms fend off all harm.'

Psalm 91:3, 4, MGE.

Be an open letter about Christ . . .
be gracious.

'You are an open letter
about Christ . . . written,
not with pen and ink but with
the Spirit of the living God,
engraved not on stone,
but on human hearts.'

2 Corinthians 3:3, Phillips.

The 'scent' of Christ's
followers is the
'scent' of grace.

'Thanks be to God who leads us, . . .
on Christ's triumphant way
and makes our knowledge of him
spread . . . like a lovely perfume!
We Christians have the
unmistakable "scent" of Christ.'

2 Corinthians 2:14, 15, Phillips.

God says, 'Love me,
love my friends who
are in need.
It's a package deal.'

' "I was hungry and you fed me,
I was thirsty and you gave me
a drink, I was homeless and
you gave me a room. . . .
Whenever you did one of these
things to someone overlooked
or ignored, that was me –
you did it to me." '

Matthew 25:35-40, MGE.

If God's grace cannot
change human nature,
nothing can.

'I have been crucified with Christ
and I no longer live, but
Christ lives in me.'

Galatians 2:20.

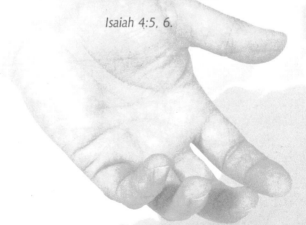

The God of grace is our refuge in adversity and the times of storm.

'Then the Lord will create over all of Mount Zion . . . a shelter and shade from the heat of the day, and a refuge and hiding place from the storm and rain.'

Isaiah 4:5, 6.

Grace is not grace unless it is gratis.

'At the present time there is
a remnant chosen by grace.
And if by grace, then it is
no longer by works;
if it were, grace would
no longer be grace.'

Romans 11:5, 6.

Those with grace do not look for praise.

' "God opposes the proud but gives grace to the humble." '

James 4:6.

Without the burden of
affliction we cannot
reach the heights
of grace.

'Think of your sufferings as
a weaning from that old sinful
habit of always expecting
to get your own way.'

1 Peter 4:1, 2, MGE.

In 'our present
sufferings'
God controls the
thermostat.

'Our present sufferings are
not worth comparing with
the glory that will be
revealed in us.'

Romans 8:18.

Theological 'rightness'
is not enough.
The difference has
got to show.
What *makes* the
difference is grace.

'If anyone is in Christ,
he is a new creation;
the old has gone,
the new has come!'

2 Corinthians 5:17.

A God of peace, grace, and miracles!

' "In me you may have peace.
In this world you will have trouble.
But take heart!
I have overcome the world." '

John 16:33.

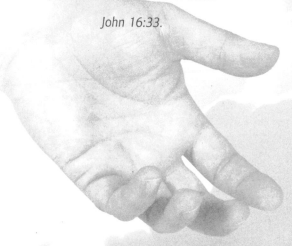

A perfectly secure place for graced people to be.

'I am convinced that neither death nor life, . . . neither angels nor demons, neither the present nor the future, nor any powers, neither height nor depth, nor anything else in all creation, will be able to separate us from the love of God that is in Christ Jesus our Lord.'

Romans 8:38, 39.

All barriers between man and man – broken down, dissolved, resolved in Jesus Christ. That is the formula of grace.

'In Christ Jesus you who once were far away have been brought near. . . .
For he himself is our peace, who has made the two one and has destroyed the barrier, the dividing wall of hostility.'

Ephesians 2:13, 14.

God has the map,
knows the way, and has
seen the weather forecast.
So just drive!

'Trust God from the
bottom of your heart;
don't try to figure out
everything on your own.
Listen for God's voice
in everything you do,
everywhere you go;
he's the one who will
keep you on track.'

Proverbs 3:5, 6, MGE.

Those who have grace
can be used by God
to transform society
and conquer the world.

'"Come!" say the Spirit
and the Bride.
Whoever hears, echo, "Come!"
Is anyone thirsty? Come!
All who will, come and drink,
Drink freely of the
Water of Life!'

Revelation 22:17, MGE.

Grace is –

God's
Riches
At
Christ's
Expense

'He is able to save completely those
who come to God through him.'

Hebrews 7:25.

The law tells you
you are crooked.
Grace straightens
you out.

'The law was given through
Moses; grace and truth came
through Jesus Christ.'

John 1:17.

Grace brings
* liberation from slavery,
* rescue from condemnation,
* resurrection from death.

We 'are justified freely by his grace
through the redemption that came
by Christ Jesus'.

Romans 3:24.

Grace-receiving Christians
are meant to be
God's workmanship,
God's masterpieces.

'For it is by grace you
have been saved. . . .
we are God's workmanship,
created in Christ Jesus.'

Ephesians 2:8, 9.

Athletes are not admitted
to the contest of virtue.
Athletics is not the point
with salvation.
The point is grace.

'Now God has us where he wants us,
with all the time in this world and
the next to shower grace and
kindness upon us in Christ Jesus.
Saving is all his idea, and all his work.
All we do is trust him enough
to let him do it.'

Ephesians 2:7-9, MGE.

The foundation words
of the Gospel are
salvation, grace and faith.
Salvation means freedom
from death and slavery.
Grace is God's free and
undeserved mercy.
Faith is the humble trust
with which we receive
it for ourselves.

'For it is by grace you have
been saved, through faith –
and this not from yourselves,
it is the gift of God.'

Ephesians 2:8.

The only qualification to
receive grace is need.
All you need to receive
the water of life is thirst!

'"Hey there! All who are thirsty,
come to the water! Are you penniless?
Come anyway – buy and eat! . . .
Buy without money –
everything's free."'

Isaiah 55:1, MGE.

The bridge to salvation
is grace – and it can
take everyone's weight.

'God, who is rich in mercy,
made us alive with Christ even
when we were dead in transgressions –
it is by grace you have been saved.'

Ephesians 2:4, 5.

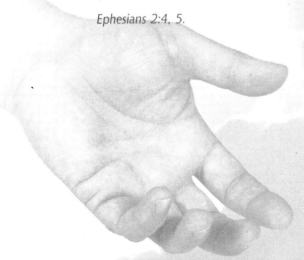

Grace was made
possible through a
rescue performed
on a cross.

'In [Jesus] we have redemption, . . .
the forgiveness of sin, in accordance
with the riches of God's grace that
he lavished on us.'

Ephesians 1:7, 8.

God cannot use you to
win until you are
winsome.
Winsome means
'having grace'.

'Grace and peace to you from God our
Father and the Lord Jesus Christ . . .
who has blessed us.'

Ephesians 1:2, 3.

God does not comfort us
to make us comfortable,
but to make us
comforters.

'God . . . is our Father and the
source of all mercy and comfort.
For he gives us comfort in all
our trials so that we in turn may
be able to give the same sort of
strong sympathy to others in their
troubles that we receive from God.'

2 Corinthians 1:3-5, Phillips.

The first evidence of a
grace-full heart is a
thankful heart.

'This is for your benefit,
so that the grace that is reaching
more and more people may
cause thanksgiving. . . .'

2 Corinthians 4:15.

Peaceful sleep comes not
from counting sheep,
but by counting on
the Shepherd.

'I will lie down and sleep in peace,
for you alone, O Lord,
make me dwell in safety.'

Psalm 4:8.

Grasping grace does not mean living happily ever after. It *does* mean living for ever.

'We are hard pressed on every side, but not crushed; . . . struck down, but not destroyed.'

2 Corinthians 4:8, 9.

You will not enter the
Kingdom of Glory unless
the Kingdom of Grace
is within you.

'The one who raised the Lord Jesus
from the dead will also raise us
with Jesus and present us with
you in his presence.'

2 Corinthians 4:14.

We are cheap clay pots
– to be filled full of the
treasures of God's grace.

'We have this treasure in jars of clay
to show that this all-surpassing power
is from God and not from us.'

2 Corinthians 4:7.

God's grace towards us
reproduces his
graciousness within us.

'Whoever sows sparingly
will also reap sparingly,
and whoever sows generously
will also reap generously.'

2 Corinthians 9:6.

Grace-blindness
is a potentially
terminal condition.

'The god of this age has blinded
the minds of unbelievers,
so that they cannot see the light of
the gospel of the glory of Christ.'

2 Corinthians 4:4.

Christ makes the difference –
and what makes the
difference *about* Christ is
his grace.

'For the sake of Christ, . . .
I am content with weaknesses,
insults, hardships, persecutions,
and calamities; for when I am weak,
then I am strong.'

Paul in 2 Corinthians 12:10, RSV

Grace grows best in the winter. . . .

' "My grace is sufficient for you, for my power is made perfect in weakness." '

2 Corinthians 12:9, RSV.

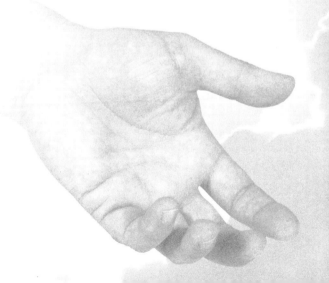

He is the Prince of Peace
because he is
the King of Grace.
Grace is the beginning,
the consummation and
the crown.

'To us a child is born,
to us a son is given. . . .
And he will be called
Wonderful Counsellor,
Mighty God, Everlasting Father,
Prince of Peace.'

Isaiah 9:6.

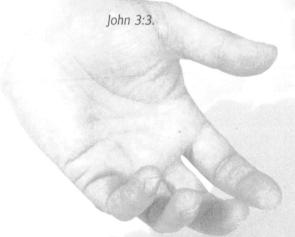

New birth comes to those who, in repentance, grasp forgiveness – and grace.

'"I tell you the truth, no one can see the kingdom of God unless he is born again."'

John 3:3.

Jesus is not just the
source of grace –
he *is* grace.

'The Word became flesh and dwelt
among us, full of grace and truth. . . .
And from his fulness have we all
received, grace upon grace.'

John 1:14-16, RSV.

The source of grace?
When God emptied
himself into Jesus.
And Jesus emptied
himself on the Cross.

'Have this mind among yourselves,
which you have in Christ Jesus, who,
though he was in the form of God, . . .
emptied himself . . .
and became obedient unto death,
even death on a cross.'

Philippians 2:5-8, RSV.

Grace

There is only one thing the Church can give to the world that the world cannot get anywhere else – and that is grace.

If the Church is not a means of grace to the world, then the Church is nothing.

What is true of the Church is true of each of its members.

We are saved by God's grace. The Bible says there is no other way to be saved.

Once we have received God's grace, we are meant to become gracious. That is where the salvation formula often fails.

The world is tired of Christians who say they have the right beliefs but in whom grace is conspicuous by its absence.

This little book is meant to prioritise grace in our attention agenda and to say –

Grasp grace!

Be gracious!

Become a channel of God's grace to a world in desperate need of it.

David Marshall

Dedication

To all who grasp grace, become gracious
and are part of the Grace Awakening in the Church
that must happen before Jesus returns.

'Grace is love that cares and stoops and rescues.'

John R. W. Stott

'Grace is not sought nor bought nor wrought.
It is a free gift of Almighty God to needy mankind.'

Billy Graham

First published in 2006
Reprinted 2007
Copyright © 2006
All rights reserved. No part of this publication
may be reproduced in any form without
prior permission from the publisher.
British Library Cataloguing in Publication Data.
A catalogue record for this book is available
from the British Library.

ISBN 1-903921-32-5

Published by
Autumn House, Grantham, England.
Printed in Thailand.

All Bible texts are taken from the New International Version
unless otherwise stated.

Other versions used:

MGE: The Message: The Bible in Contemporary English.
Eugene H. Peterson (NavPress)

NLT: New Living Translation (Tyndale House)

Phillips: The New Testament in Modern English (Harper Collins)

RSV: Revised Standard Version (Collins)

God's
little book of
Grace

by

David Marshall

D1393013